SAUCES MADE

SIMPLY

SAUCES
MADE SIMPLY

70 OF THE MOST POPULAR SAUCE RECIPES

FROM THE SAUCE AND GRAVY CHANNEL

JOHNNY MAC

Legal Disclaimer:

The information contained in this cookbook is for general informational purposes only. The author and publisher of this cookbook are not responsible for any adverse reactions, effects, or consequences resulting from the use of the recipes or information contained herein. Readers are advised to use their best judgment and to consult with a qualified healthcare professional or nutritionist before making any decisions based on the content of this cookbook.

While every effort has been made to ensure the accuracy and completeness of the information in this cookbook, the author and publisher assume no responsibility for errors, inaccuracies, or omissions. The recipes provided are based on the author's personal experiences and culinary expertise, and individual results may vary.

The author and publisher do not endorse any specific brands, products, or services mentioned in this cookbook unless explicitly stated. Mention of such items is for illustrative purposes only and does not constitute an endorsement or recommendation.

The recipes in this cookbook may include allergens or ingredients that could cause adverse reactions in certain individuals. It is the responsibility of the reader to be aware of and accommodate any dietary restrictions, allergies, or health concerns. The author and publisher are not liable for any damages or harm arising from the use of this cookbook.

By using this cookbook, readers agree to release, indemnify, and hold harmless the author and publisher from any and all claims, liabilities, or expenses arising from the use or misuse of the information contained herein.

For personalized advice, readers are encouraged to consult with a qualified professional (including but not limited to your doctor, attorney, financial advisor or such other advisor as needed).

For permission requests, contact the author at thesauceandgravychannel@gmail.com

To my greatest inspirations, Christelle and Zachary.

This cookbook is a tribute to the two who make every recipe an adventure. In the kitchen where love and flavor intertwine, your encouragement, enthusiasm and joy infuse each creation with a special magic.

May these sauce recipes spread the warmth, love, and joy that you bring to my culinary journey.

TABLE OF CONTENTS

How To Use This Book

Navigating through the innovative features of this cookbook is as easy as pie! Each recipe is accompanied by a QR code and a URL link, seamlessly integrating traditional cooking with modern technology. To embark on your culinary journey, simply grab your smartphone or tablet and scan the QR code provided next to each recipe. Alternatively, you can type the URL into your computer's web browser. This will lead you to a high-definition step-by-step video tutorial, where you can watch Johnny Mac demonstrate the recipe from start to finish. After gaining insights and inspiration from the video, return to the written recipe in the comfort of your home kitchen. With detailed instructions and handy tips at your fingertips, you can confidently recreate the sauce, infusing it with your personal touch. Whether you're a seasoned chef or just starting out, this cookbook combines the convenience of technology with the satisfaction of traditional cooking, ensuring that every meal is a delightful experience.

Here's an explanation on how to scan and use a QR code to watch a video recipe:

To access the video tutorial for each recipe, simply scan the QR code provided with your smartphone or tablet. If you don't already have a QR code scanner app, you can easily download one from your device's app store. Once the app is installed, open it and point your device's camera at the QR code. The app will automatically recognize the code and prompt you to open the corresponding video link. With just a tap of your finger, you'll be transported to "The Sauce and Gravy Channel" on YouTube where Johnny Mac will guide you through the sauce-making process step-by-step. It's like having a personal cooking coach right in your own home!

INTRODUCTION

In the realm of culinary arts, sauces reign supreme as the unsung heroes, wielding the power to transform ordinary dishes into extraordinary culinary experiences. This comprehensive recipe book is your passport to the enchanting world of sauces, where each page unveils the secrets behind classic staples, innovative twists, and comforting holiday favorites.

Sauces are not mere accompaniments; they are the alchemists of flavor, the artists of texture, and the architects of memorable dining encounters. With an unparalleled ability to enhance, balance, and accentuate the natural flavors of ingredients, these liquid marvels provide a multifaceted sensory experience that lingers on the palate. Beyond gustatory pleasure, sauces bring cultural richness and diversity to the table, serving as culinary ambassadors that reflect the unique tastes and traditions of different regions around the globe.

What sets 'Sauces Made Simply' apart is my commitment to making your culinary journey seamless and enjoyable. Each sauce recipe is accompanied by a free video tutorial, offering a visual guide to help you achieve the best consistency and flavor profile. Whether you're a seasoned chef or a kitchen novice, these step-by-step videos empower you to confidently craft exquisite sauces that will leave your taste buds dancing with delight.

Join me on this culinary adventure, where each page is an invitation to explore, experiment, and savor the magic of sauces. Unleash your inner chef, recognize the transformative essence of sauces, and let the symphony of flavors redefine your culinary repertoire. The world of 'Sauces Made Simply' awaits, where sauces are not just condiments but the heartbeat of exceptional dining experiences.

Visit The Sauce and Gravy Channel on YouTube, Instagram, and The Sauce and Gravy Channel website. To be notified when a new video tutorial is released, be sure to subscribe to the YouTube channel with the "All notifications" bell. See you there!

THE BASICS

Explore the world of home-cooked excellence by unraveling the secrets of two fundamental sauces, laying the foundation for a myriad of culinary wonders: the adaptable Basic White Sauce and the flavorful Espagnole Sauce (Brown Sauce).

In your home kitchen, the Basic White Sauce acts as a versatile canvas, setting the stage for a range of delightful creations from creamy Alfredo to indulgent cheese sauces. Mastering this sauce unlocks a world of possibilities, establishing it as a key player in your culinary toolkit.

Discover rich flavors with Espagnole Sauce, a robust foundation that brings depth and sophistication to your dishes. Whether enhancing stews, gravies, or crafting a luxurious demi-glace, mastering Espagnole elevates your home-cooked meals to new heights.

These two base sauces aren't merely recipes; they are the cornerstone of countless savory adventures, providing you, the home cook, with the essential building blocks to create a symphony of flavors in your own kitchen. Get ready to explore, experiment, and savor the transformative power of these foundational sauces!

BASIC WHITE SAUCE

Makes 1 cup or 250ml

Ingredients:

1.5 tbsp or 21g unsalted butter

1.5 tbsp or 12g all-purpose flour

1 cup or 250ml heavy cream (cold)

Pinch of white pepper

Pinch of salt

Melt butter in a saucepan over low to medium heat.

Whisk in the flour, cook stirring frequently for 2 minutes.

Pour in the heavy cream, stir well to mix it into the liquid, and make sure to scrape the sides and bottom of the pan to incorporate all the butter and flour mixture (the roux).

Add the white pepper and salt, and cook until the sauce is as thick as you would like or coats the back of the spoon.

Once the sauce is thick, taste it to see if you need to adjust the seasoning. Add more salt or white pepper as needed.

Recipe video tutorial

https://youtu.be/znXbtr-6adU

ESPAGNOLE SAUCE (Basic Brown Sauce)

Makes 1 ½ cups or 375ml

Ingredients:

1/4 cup or 56g clarified or melted unsalted butter

1/4 cup or 32g all-purpose flour

5 cups or 1250ml beef stock

1/4 cup or 60g tomato sauce

8 black peppercorns

1 bay leaf

Few sprigs of thyme

4 parsley stems

Add the clarified or melted butter into a saucepan over medium heat.

Whisk the flour into the clarified butter to create a roux. Cook the roux mixture over medium heat for 10 minutes or until it turns a brown paper bag color. Stir the roux frequently and watch the heat. Turn it down if it becomes too hot. You don't want to burn the roux.

Over medium heat, stir a cool beef stock into the hot roux. Scrape the bottom and sides of the pot to fully incorporate all the roux into the stock.

Once well mixed, add the tomato sauce, peppercorns, and bouquet garni (bay leaf, thyme and parsley stems). Bring the sauce to a simmer over medium to medium-high heat. Then lower the heat and reduce the sauce by half for 1 to 1.5 hours.

Skim the top of the sauce to remove the foam and impurities throughout the reduction process.

When the sauce has been reduced, turn off the heat and strain it through a fine sieve into a clean saucepot or bowl.

Recipe video tutorial

https://youtu.be/iHo68R9eQtl

SAUCE FOR CHICKEN

Step into the enticing realm of sauces crafted to enhance the delightful appeal of chicken. This chapter invites you to explore a captivating interplay of flavors, textures, and aromas that transform the ordinary into the extraordinary. Whether you savor the comforting embrace of a classic white sauce, the vibrant zest of a Cajun gravy, or the velvety indulgence of a creamy suprême sauce, this diverse collection of sauces caters to every culinary inclination. From timeless classics to innovative blends, these recipes inspire you to uncover the transformative potential of sauces in the world of chicken cuisine. Immerse yourself in a culinary adventure where each saucy creation offers an opportunity to reimagine and relish the essence of chicken in unexpected ways.

CAJUN GRAVY

Makes about 2 cups or 500ml

Ingredients:

2 tbsp or 28g unsalted butter

1/3 cup or 35g celery stalk finely chopped

1/2 cup or 60g onion minced

1/4 cup or 35g red bell pepper finely chopped

2 cloves of minced garlic

1 tbsp or 15g bacon grease

2 tbsp or 16g all-purpose flour

1.5 cups or 375ml veal or beef stock

1/4 tsp Worcestershire sauce

Dash of Tabasco sauce

1 tbsp Cajun spice mix (homemade recipe below)

1/2 tsp oregano

1/2 tsp thyme

Homemade Cajun spice mix:

2 tbsp paprika, 1.5 tbsp ground thyme, 1 tbsp garlic powder, 1 tbsp celery salt, 2 tsp cayenne pepper, 2 tsp white pepper, 2 tsp black pepper

Melt 1 tbsp or 14g of butter in a saucepan over medium heat and add the celery, onion and red pepper. Sauté the vegetables for 10 minutes or until soft and tender. Then add garlic to the pan and cook for 1 minute.

Remove the vegetables and garlic from the pan. Using the same pan, melt 1 tbsp or 14g of butter and bacon grease over medium heat.

Whisk in the flour. Stir and cook over low to medium heat for 10 minutes or until the mixture is a brown paper bag color.

Add the vegetable and garlic back to the pan. Mix and slowly cook on low to medium heat for 5 minutes.

Pour the veal stock into pan while whisking over medium heat. Be sure to scrape the sides and bottom of the pan.

Add the Worcestershire, Tabasco sauce, oregano, thyme and 1 tbsp of Cajun spice mix. Give the gravy a stir, bring to a simmer over low to medium heat and cook until the gravy becomes thick.

Taste the gravy and add salt and pepper if needed.

Recipe video tutorial

https://youtu.be/jUOoPCRRZvE

BELL PEPPER GRAVY

Serves 2 to 4

Ingredients:

1 tbsp or 15ml neutral oil

1 lb. or 500g chicken

1 red bell pepper diced

1 green bell pepper diced

2 tbsp chopped parsley

1 clove of garlic minced

1/4 cup or 60ml sherry

3 tbsp or 42g unsalted butter

3 tbsp or 24g all-purpose flour

2 cups or 500ml chicken broth

Dash of salt and pepper

2 tbsp chopped parsley

Add the neutral oil to a saucepan over medium to high heat. Season the chicken with salt and pepper and fry it in the pan until completely cooked through. Remove the chicken from the pan, add the bell peppers to the pan and cook until they are lightly browned. Stir in the minced garlic, cook for 1 minute.

Deglaze the pan with the sherry, reduce until it's almost all gone.

Make a well in the center of the pan, add the butter and let it melt. Sprinkle the flour, mix and cook for roughly 2 to 3 minutes.

Pour chicken broth into the pan, stir and cook uncovered over medium heat until thick.

Place the cooked chicken back into the pan, simmer for a few minutes to warm it back up and infuse flavor.

Taste the sauce, add salt and black pepper if needed.

Turn off the heat, stir in the parsley and enjoy!

Recipe video tutorial

https://youtu.be/ogkz4n7A44Q

CREAMED CHICKEN

Serves 2 to 4

Ingredients:

3 tbsp or 42g unsalted butter

1 onion or 185g

3 tbsp or 24g all-purpose flour

1 cup or 250ml chicken stock

1 cup or 250ml milk

1 cooked shredded chicken breast or 205g

1/2 cup cooked carrots

1/2 cup cooked peas

Pepper to taste

Dash of salt

To a saucepan over medium to high heat, add 1 tbsp or 14g butter and melt it down. Add the chopped onions and cook until tender.

Move the onions to the sides of the pan, making a well in the center. Add the remaining 2 tbsp or 28g of butter to the center of the pan and melt it down

Add the flour to the melted butter, reduce the heat to low to medium. Use a spatula to mix the flour into the butter, then combine the butter mixture with the onions. Stir and cook for 2 to 3 minutes.

Pour in the chicken stock, stir well to incorporate the butter, flour and onions into the liquid.

Add the milk, shredded chicken, peas, carrots and black pepper. Reduce the sauce down over low to medium heat for 5 to 10 minutes or until thick. Be sure to stir occasionally.

Give the sauce a taste. Add salt and more pepper if needed.

Recipe video tutorial

https://youtu.be/lZEzSX8TFUg

CREAMY LEEK SAUCE

Makes 1 cup or 250ml

Ingredients:

2 leeks- the light green section, with a little white (roughly 1 cup)

3 tbsp or 42g unsalted butter

1/4 cup or 63ml chicken stock

1 cup or 250ml heavy cream

1/2 tsp chervil

1/4 tsp salt

1/4 tsp white pepper

Make a slice down the center of the leeks. Start the cut an inch or two from the bottom (root side) moving up to the top (green leafy part). This will open the leeks so they can be washed to remove the dirt and grime.

After washing the leeks, cut out the middle sections to keep the light green and slightly white areas. Julienne the leeks – cut it into 2-inch long, thin strips.

To make the sauce:

Add the butter to a saucepan over medium heat, melt it down, and add the leeks. Stir to coat the leeks with the butter. Cook until tender – approximately 2 minutes.

Pour chicken stock into the pan and reduce by 3/4th. Then add heavy cream, chervil, salt and white pepper. Mix and bring to a simmer. Lower the heat and reduce until the sauce becomes thick and coats the back of a spoon.

Recipe video tutorial

https://youtu.be/robDpvASnSM

FAST CHICKEN NUGGET DIPPING SAUCE

Makes 3/4 cup or 187ml

Ingredients:

1/2 cup or 125ml mayonnaise

1 tbsp or 15g BBQ sauce (see page 78 for a KC-style BBQ sauce recipe)

1 tsp yellow mustard

1 tbsp or 15g honey

Add all the ingredients to a bowl, mix and dip away!

Recipe video tutorial

https://youtu.be/bCanepdjMQg

ALABAMA WHITE SAUCE

Makes 1 ¼ cups or 313ml

Ingredients:

1 cup or 250ml mayonnaise

1/2 tsp onion powder

1 tsp garlic powder

1 tsp black pepper

1/2 tsp salt

2 tsp Dijon mustard

2 tsp Worcestershire sauce

1/4 cup or 63ml apple cider vinegar

1/4 tsp hot sauce (ex: Tabasco)

Add all the ingredients to a bowl, mix and enjoy!

Recipe video tutorial

https://youtu.be/bRKefptkwE4

HOMEMADE KFC-STYLE GRAVY

Makes 1 ¼ cups or 313ml

Ingredients:

2 tbsp or 28g unsalted butter

2 tbsp or 16g all-purpose flour

1 cup or 250ml chicken stock

1.5 cups or 375ml brown veal or beef stock

1 tbsp of the secret spice mixture

1 tbsp or 15ml white wine vinegar

Secret spice mixture:

1 tsp each of: paprika, dried basil, dried sage, garlic powder, onion powder, dried coriander, dried marjoram, cayenne pepper, oregano, black pepper, and sea salt

To make the secret spice mix:

Add all the secret spices to a mortar and pestle and grind to create a fine powder.

To make the gravy:

Add the butter to a saucepan over medium heat, melt (for additional taste, the butter can be cooked longer and browned), and whisk in the flour. Cook for at least 2 to 3 minutes (the butter and flour mixture can be cooked longer and browned if wanted).

Pour in the chicken stock, veal stock, and add the secret spice mix. Whisk and bring to a simmer over medium to high heat. Then turn the heat to low and reduce until thick.

Skim the top of the gravy to remove the impurities while reducing it down.

At the tail end of the reduction process (when the gravy is as thick as you like), add the white wine vinegar, stir and cook for an additional 1 minute.

Taste the gravy. Add salt or pepper as needed.

Recipe video tutorial

https://youtu.be/pO0bO4ITQkc

SUPRÊME SAUCE

Makes 1 ¾ cups or 438ml

Ingredients:

3 tbsp or 42g unsalted butter

3 tbsp or 24g all-purpose flour

2.5 cups or 625ml chicken stock

1 cup or 250ml heavy cream

Salt and white pepper to taste

Melt the butter in a saucepan over medium heat. Be sure not to brown the butter or add color to it.

Mix flour into the melted butter with a whisk or spatula. Cook for 2 minutes, stir frequently to ensure the roux (flour and butter mixture) cooks evenly.

Pour chicken stock into the pan. Mix well with a whisk or spoon. Scrape the sides and bottom of the pan to incorporate all the roux into the sauce. Bring to a simmer over medium heat. Once the sauce simmers, turn the heat to low and reduce slowly for 10 minutes or until thick.

Add heavy cream, increase the heat to medium to medium-high, bring to a simmer then turn the heat down and reduce the sauce until thick – coats the back of a spoon.

Taste the sauce and add salt and pepper if needed.

Tip:

Skim the foamy impurities off the top of the sauce during the reduction process to keep the sauce pure and clean.

Recipe video tutorial

https://youtu.be/adKQpeYG-Qg

VELOUTÉ SAUCE

Makes 1 ½ cups or 375ml

Ingredients:

3 tbsp or 42g unsalted butter

3 tbsp or 24g all-purpose flour

2 cups or 500ml chicken stock

1/4 tsp salt

1/4 tsp white pepper

Add the butter to a saucepan over medium heat and melt it down. If you would like to give it a light blonde color, you can (just cook it a little longer).

Once the butter has melted, whisk in the flour to make a roux.

Cook the roux for 2 to 3 minutes, frequently stirring until you smell a warm nutty smell.

Pour cool chicken stock into the hot roux, whisk the mixture to thoroughly combine. Make sure to scrape the sides and bottom of the pan to ensure the roux is well incorporated into the stock.

Bring to a simmer and reduce over low heat for roughly 15 minutes or until the sauce is to the desired thickness. Skim/remove the foamy impurities that may build up on the top of the sauce while reducing.

(Optional) When the sauce is as thick as you like, strain it through a fine sieve into a clean saucepan to guarantee you have a silky-smooth sauce.

Taste the sauce and adjust the seasoning. Add salt and white pepper if needed.

Tips:

How to know when a roux is done cooking: the color around bubbles turns from butter yellow to a light white. Another indicator is that the roux starts to release a warm nutty smell.

Recipe video tutorial

https://youtu.be/EIC5MQYpNIg

PANTRY-STYLE TERIYAKI SAUCE

Makes 1 ½ cups or 375ml

Ingredients:

4 garlic cloves or roughly 12g

1/2 cup or 100g light brown sugar

1 cup or 250ml low sodium soy sauce (If you don't have low sodium soy, you can dilute regular soy with water. Dilute it to your taste or half water half soy.)

2 tbsp or 30ml rice vinegar

1/2 tsp ground ginger

2 tsp or 10ml sesame oil

3 tbsp or 24g cornstarch

4 tbsp or 60ml water

1 tbsp sesame seeds

To a saucepan, add light brown sugar, soy sauce, rice vinegar, ground ginger, minced garlic, and sesame oil. Mix well and turn the burner to medium to high heat. Bring to a light boil and simmer for 1 minute.

Make a cornstarch slurry: add the cornstarch to a small bowl, pour in the water, and stir.

After the sauce has simmered for 1 minute, add half the cornstarch slurry to the sauce, and bring it to a light simmer. Check the sauce for thickness. If it is not as thick as you like, add more of the cornstarch slurry, simmer - repeat this process until the sauce is as thick as you would like. Please note that, when the sauce is hot, it will be relatively thin Once it cools off, it will be thicker.

(Optional) Toast sesame seeds by adding them to a sauté pan over medium to high heat. Stir frequently. Once they start to turn light brown, take them off heat and add them to the sauce. Stir and you're ready to serve.

Tips:

For a thinner sauce, use less of the cornstarch slurry.

To reduce the salt level, thin out the soy sauce with water.

Recipe video tutorial

https://youtu.be/ZqV05-ltEDs

SAUCE FOR STEAK

Immerse yourself in the sizzling and savory realm of sauces, embark on a culinary journey delving into the art of enhancing one of the most celebrated meats: steak. In this chapter, explore a world where flavors converge to complement the robust and mouthwatering character of steak. From the classic elegance of a red wine reduction to the bold kick of a green peppercorn sauce, this collection caters to every steak lover's palate. Whether you lean towards the simple richness of a Japanese style Yakiniku dipping sauce or the velvety decadence of a Béarnaise, these sauces are poised to elevate your steak experience to new heights. Join the exploration of the diverse spectrum of steak sauces, where each recipe adds a unique flavor profile to turn a simple steak into a culinary masterpiece. Get ready to tantalize your taste buds and elevate your steak dinners with the perfect saucy accompaniment.

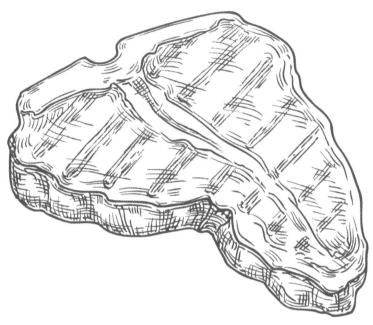

BLENDER BÉARNAISE SAUCE

Makes 1 ¼ cups or 313ml

Ingredients:

10 tbsp or 140g melted unsalted butter

1 chopped shallot

1/2 tbsp tarragon

1/2 tbsp chervil

1 tsp cracked black pepper

1/4 cup or 63ml white wine – Chardonnay

1/4 cup or 63ml white wine vinegar

1 to 2 tbsp or 15 to 30ml water

3 egg yolks

1 tbsp or 15ml lemon juice

1/4 tsp salt

1/8 tsp cayenne pepper

Add the butter to a saucepan over medium heat and melt it down – you want the temperature to be roughly 140 ° F or 60° C.

To another saucepan, add the chopped shallot, tarragon, chervil, black pepper, white wine and white wine vinegar. Stir, bring to a simmer and reduce until the liquid is almost all gone.

To a blender, add the egg yolks, the reduced shallot and herb mixture from the saucepan, lemon juice, salt and cayenne pepper. Quickly blend until the mixture turns from yellow to a pale yellow – roughly 20 to 30 seconds. (Optional) Add a little water if your blender is having a hard time mixing. The water should help the ingredients reach the blades.

Once the sauce is a pale-yellow color, slowly drizzle the warm melted butter in the blender over medium speed. Blend for roughly 30 seconds or until the sauce becomes thick.

Recipe video tutorial

https://youtu.be/OItJ3Q_tKSA

BRANDY CREAM SAUCE

Makes 1 cup or 250ml

Ingredients:

Steak of your choice

3 tbsp or 42g unsalted butter

1 tbsp or 15ml neutral oil

1/2 shallot finely diced

Few sprigs of fresh thyme

1/4 cup or 63ml Brandy

1/2 cup or 125ml Espagnole sauce (see page 16) or demi-glace

1/2 cup or 125ml heavy cream

Salt and pepper to taste

To cook the steak:

To a pan, add 1 tbsp or 14g of butter and the neutral oil. Melt it over medium to high heat. Pat the steak dry, season with salt and pepper or seasonings of your choice. When the pan/butter/oil are hot, add the steak, sear both sides, drop in a few thyme sprigs – add additional butter if needed, baste and cook to your liking. Remove the steak from the pan, cover it and let it rest in a warm place.

To make the sauce:

(Optional) Degrease the pan by removing the excess fat (If you want to use the fat to sauté the shallots, you can). Don't clean the bits and pieces from the pan – leave them and a small amount of steak fat. Melt 1 tbsp or 14g butter, add the diced shallots, and cook until tender.

Deglaze the pan by adding the Brandy. With a spatula or spoon, scrape the sides and bottom of the pan to release all the bits and pieces up into the liquid. Reduce the Brandy until it is nearly all gone.

Add a few sprigs of thyme and an Espagnole sauce or demi-glace. Stir, bring to a simmer, and cook for 1 to 2 minutes to infuse flavor.

Pour in heavy cream, stir, bring to a simmer over medium heat. Reduce the sauce for 3 to 5 minutes or until it is as thick as you would like. You will know the sauce is done when you stir and can see trails (you can see the bottom of the pan) or the sauce coats the back of a spoon.

Take the sauce off heat, remove the thyme sprigs,

stir in 1 tbsp or 14g cold butter with a spoon or spatula.

Taste the sauce and see if you need to add salt or black pepper.

Recipe video tutorial

https://youtu.be/3CC7SmTzXiE

CHIMICHURRI SAUCE

Makes 1 cup or 250ml

Ingredients:

1 cup of flat-leaf parsley

2 tbsp oregano

5 garlic cloves

1/4 tsp red pepper flakes

1/2 tsp salt

1/4 tsp black pepper

1/2 cup or 125ml extra virgin olive oil

2 tbsp or 30ml red wine vinegar

Remove the parsley and oregano leaves from their stems. Finely chop the leaves and add them to a glass container/jar.

Finely mince the garlic cloves and place them into the jar.

Add red pepper flakes, salt, black pepper, olive oil and red wine vinegar to the jar.

Shake or stir and enjoy.

Recipe video tutorial

https://youtu.be/SbTQMa9EaRo

GREEN PEPPERCORN SAUCE

Makes 1 cup or 250ml

Ingredients:

Steak of your choice

3 tbsp or 42g unsalted butter

1 tbsp or 15ml neutral oil

2 tbsp or 35g green peppercorns

3 tbsp or 45ml Cognac

3/4 cup or 187ml Espagnole sauce (see page 16) or demi-glace

3/4 cup or 187ml heavy cream

To cook the steak:

Melt 1 tbsp or 14g butter along with the neutral oil in a pan over medium to high heat. Pat the steak dry, season with salt and pepper. When the pan is hot, add the steak, sear both sides, drop in a few herbs if you would like (thyme, rosemary...) – add additional butter if needed, baste and cook the steak to your liking. Remove the steak from the pan, cover it and let it rest in a warm place.

To make the sauce:

(Optional) Degrease the pan by removing the excess fat. Don't clean the pan – leave the bits and pieces and a small amount of steak fat in the pan.

Melt 1 tbsp or 14g butter over medium heat, use a spoon or spatula to scrape the pan to release the bits and pieces of steak into the melted butter.

Add the green peppercorns and mix them into the butter.

Remove the pan from the burner (turn burner off), pour in the Cognac – carefully light the Cognac on fire. Make sure there is nothing over, around, or anywhere near the pan. You don't want to catch anything on fire. Once the fire dies out, return the pan to a burner over medium heat. Reduce any remaining Cognac down until it is almost all gone.

Add the Espagnole sauce to the pan, bring to a simmer and cook for 1 to 2 minutes.

Pour in the heavy cream, stir, bring to a simmer and reduce down by half or until it's as thick as you would like. Occasionally smash a green peppercorn or two to add flavor.

Take the sauce off heat and mount it with butter by adding 1 tbsp or 14g cold butter. Stir with a spoon.

Taste and adjust the seasoning with salt and pepper if needed.

Recipe video tutorial

https://youtu.be/EMZk79fpCeY

MADEIRA WINE SAUCE

Makes 1 cup or 250ml

Ingredients:

3 tbsp or 42g unsalted butter (2 tbsp or 28g cut into cubes and kept cold)

1 finely minced shallot

1 cup or 250ml Madeira wine

1.5 oz or 42.5g pack of beef or veal demi-glace

1 cup or 250ml beef broth

Place 1 tbsp or 14g butter in a saucepan over medium to high heat and melt it down.

Add the minced shallot and cook it until tender (you should see a touch of brown around the edges).

Deglaze the pan by adding Madeira wine, stir, bring to a simmer and reduce it by 3/4th.

Add the demi-glace to the pan and whisk it into the Madeira mixture. Then pour in the beef broth. Stir and bring the sauce back to a simmer, reduce until it's as thick as you would like.

Take the sauce off heat, add 2 tbsp or 28g of cubed cold butter, and mix it in by swirling it in the pan or stirring with a spoon.

Taste the sauce and add salt and pepper if needed.

Recipe video tutorial

https://youtu.be/166MJtDM3L8

MUSHROOM GRAVY

Makes 1 ½ cups or 375ml

Ingredients:

4 tbsp or 56g unsalted butter

1 tbsp or 15ml neutral oil

8oz or 227g button mushrooms chopped

2 sprigs of fresh thyme

3 tbsp or 24g all-purpose flour

2 cups or 500ml beef broth

1 tsp soy sauce

1/2 tsp granulated sugar

1 tsp Dijon mustard

To a saucepan over high heat, add 1 tbsp or 14g of butter and the neutral oil. Once the butter starts to brown, add the mushrooms. When tender, add the sprigs of fresh thyme. Turn the heat to medium and cook until golden brown.

Make a well in the center of the pan (moving the mushrooms to the sides) and add 3 tbsp or 42g of butter. Melt it down over medium heat. Then add the flour on top of the butter. Mix the flour into the butter first, then combine with the mushrooms and cook for 2 to 3 minutes.

Pour in the beef broth, stir scraping the sides and bottom of the pan to release any bits into the liquid. Add the soy sauce, bring to a simmer over medium heat, and reduce down until the sauce is as thick as you would like.

Once thick, remove the thyme sprigs from the pan. Turn the heat to low, add the sugar and Dijon mustard, and mix. To incorporate the mustard into to the sauce, I would recommend using a whisk.

Taste and adjust the seasoning as needed by adding salt and pepper.

Recipe video tutorial

https://youtu.be/XSGEwqycung

46

MUSHROOM RED WINE SAUCE

Makes 2 cups or 500ml

Ingredients:

Steak of your choice

2 tbsp or 30ml neutral oil

3/4 lb. or 375g sliced button mushrooms

1 medium diced shallot or 40g

6 sprigs of fresh thyme

2 cups or 500ml red wine (ex: Merlot, Cabernet)

2 tbsp beef or veal demi-glace

7 tbsp or 98g unsalted butter (6 tbsp or 84g should be cubed and cold)

Salt and pepper to taste

To cook the steak:

Melt 1 tbsp or 14g of butter with 1 tbsp or 15ml of neutral oil in a pan over medium to high heat. Pat the steak dry, season with salt and pepper. When the pan is hot, add the steak, sear both sides, drop in a few herbs (thyme, rosemary, garlic…). Add additional butter if needed. Baste and cook the steak to your liking. Remove the steak from the pan, cover it, and let it rest in a warm place.

To make the sauce:

Pour 1 tbsp or 15ml of neutral oil in to the pan over medium to high heat. Don't clean the pan - leave the bits and pieces and a small amount of steak fat in the pan. When the oil is hot, add the mushrooms and stir. Once tender, add the shallots and thyme, and stir. Cook until the mushrooms have a touch of brown and the shallots are soft.

Deglaze the pan by adding red wine. Stir, mix in the demi-glace, and reduce the sauce down over medium heat by half or until it's as thick as you would like.

Remove the thyme sprigs from the pan. Turn off the heat. Mount the sauce with 6 tbsp or 84g of cubed cold butter. Add the butter to the pan a few pieces at a time. Stir it in with a spoon or swirl the pan. Once melted, add more butter and repeat the process until it has all mixed into the sauce.

Taste and adjust the seasoning with salt and pepper if needed.

Recipe video tutorial

https://youtu.be/yG9zrLwu39A

RED WINE SAUCE

Makes 1/3 cup or 83ml

Ingredients:

Steak of your choice

2 tbsp or 28g unsalted butter

1 tbsp or 15ml neutral oil

2 tbsp or 30g finely diced onion

2 cloves of minced garlic

1/2 cup or 125ml of red wine

1 tsp honey

2 tsp Dijon mustard

1 tsp thyme

Salt and pepper to taste

To cook the steak:

Melt 1 tbsp or 14g butter and 1 tbsp or 15ml of neutral oil in a pan over medium to high heat. Pat the steak dry, season with salt and pepper. When the pan is hot, add the steak, sear both sides, drop in a few herbs (thyme, rosemary, garlic...) – add additional butter if needed. Baste and cook the steak to your liking. Remove the steak from the pan, cover it, and let it rest in a warm place.

To make the sauce:

Add the onion and garlic to the pan you cooked the steak in. Cook until tender.

Pour in the wine and add the honey, mustard, and thyme. Stir, bring to a simmer and reduce by 2/3rd or until thick.

Turn the heat off and mount the sauce with butter by adding 1 tbsp or 14g of cold butter. Stir with a spoon.

Taste and adjust the seasoning with salt and pepper if needed.

Recipe video tutorial

https://youtu.be/SfsEMMadAHk

SESAME SEED YAKINIKU SAUCE

Makes 1/2 cup or 125ml

Ingredients:

1/4 cup or 63ml soy sauce

2 tbsp or 30ml mirin

2 tsp sesame oil

1 clove minced garlic

2.5 tbsp or 35g granulated white sugar

2 tsp or 12g sesame seeds

Add 1.5 tsp or 9g sesame seeds to a mortar and pestle, lightly grind them.

To a saucepan, add the remaining 1/2 tsp or 3g sesame seeds and toast them over medium to high heat. Remove them and place to the side for later.

To make the sauce:

Add soy sauce, mirin, sesame oil, garlic, and granulated white sugar to a small saucepan. Turn the heat to medium, stir, bring to a gentle simmer, cook for 3 minutes.

Remove the sauce from heat, let it sit for at least 10 minutes to infuse the flavors.

Strain the sauce into a glass jar or mixing bowl.

Add the ground and toasted sesame seeds, mix and enjoy.

Recipe video tutorial

https://youtu.be/QhlcnXQ8LT8

SAUCE FOR FISH

In this chapter, explore a myriad of sauces designed to elevate the bounty of oceans and lakes to new heights on your plate. From the vibrant freshness of a mango-infused salsa to the classic sophistication of a parsley and lemon sauce, this collection spans a spectrum of tastes that harmonize seamlessly with different fish varieties. Whether you prefer a quick fish taco sauce or the subtle richness of a beurre blanc, these sauces are crafted to enhance, not overpower, the unique essence of each fish dish. Discover the art of saucing for fish, where each recipe promises to transform your fish dining experience into a symphony of flavors. Get ready to embark on a culinary journey that celebrates the diverse, delectable nuances of fish, beautifully complemented by the perfect sauce.

5-MINUTE HOLLANDAISE SAUCE

Makes 1 ¼ cups or 313ml

Ingredients:

10 tbsp or 140g unsalted butter

3 large egg yolks

1 tbsp or 15ml lemon Juice (half a squeezed lemon – use more if you like a stronger lemon taste or if you want a thinner sauce)

1/4 tsp of salt

1/8 tsp cayenne pepper

Add butter to a saucepan over low to medium heat and melt it down.

Separate the yolk from 3 large eggs, place them into a blender along with the lemon, salt and cayenne pepper.

Blend the mixture on low for roughly a minute until the sauce turns a light-yellow color.

While the blender is still on low, slowly drizzle the hot, melted butter in. Blend for 15 to 30 seconds - until the sauce emulsifies and becomes thick.

Tips:

If the sauce is too thick, you can thin it out with lemon juice or water.

The melted butter should be roughly 140° F or 60° C.

Recipe video tutorial

https://youtu.be/NDnFKU6_hVU

BEURRE BLANC

Makes 1/2 cup or 125ml

Ingredients:

White fish of your choice

1 tbsp or 15ml neutral oil

1 small shallot finely chopped

1 tbsp or 15ml white wine vinegar

5 tbsp or 75ml white wine

2 tbsp or 30ml heavy cream

1/2 cup or 114g unsalted butter cut into cubes – keep cold

Salt and pepper to taste

(Optional) Fry the fish in a pan using the neutral oil. Remove the fish and put in a warm place. Use this pan to make the sauce. Make sure to leave any bits and pieces of the fish on the bottom of the pan – this will add a delicious flavor.

If you did not fry the fish in the pan or if the pan looks dry after frying your fish, add 1 tbsp of neutral oil. Drop in the chopped shallot, stir and cook until tender.

Deglaze the pan with white wine vinegar and white wine over medium heat. Reduce until the liquid is almost all gone. Use a spoon or spatula to scrape the bottom of the pan to release all the bits and pieces.

Add the heavy cream. Bring to a simmer and then turn off the heat.

Place the cubed cold butter into the pan in batches, adding few pieces at a time. Use a spoon or spatula to stir and emulsify (combine) the butter into the sauce.

Tips:

Keep the butter cold until used. This will help it to emulsify better into the sauce.

If the sauce has too much of a strong acidic taste, add a little more butter.

Recipe video tutorial

https://youtu.be/iPnJm4UbQJc

FISH TACO SAUCE

Makes about 3/4 cup or 187ml

Ingredients:

1/2 cup or 125g sour cream

1/3 cup or 83ml mayonnaise

1 tsp garlic powder

1 tsp chopped cilantro

2 tbsp or 30ml lime juice

1 tsp Sriracha chili sauce (if you like it spicy, add more)

Add all the ingredients to a bowl, mix and serve.

Recipe video tutorial

https://youtu.be/WXGB62T6bWQ

FISHERMAN'S DEVILED SAUCE

Makes 1 ¼ cups or 313ml

Ingredients:

1/2 cup or 114g unsalted butter

1 tbsp or 15ml Worcestershire sauce

1/2 cup or 125g ketchup

1 tbsp or 15g onions minced

1 small garlic clove minced

1 tsp parsley finely chopped

1 tsp tarragon finely chopped

1 tsp chives finely chopped

1 tsp Dijon mustard

Dash of ground thyme

Dash of Tabasco sauce

Salt and pepper to taste

To a saucepan over medium heat, add the butter and slowly melt it down.

Add Worcestershire sauce and ketchup and mix. Then, add the minced onions, garlic, chopped parsley, tarragon, chives, Dijon mustard, ground thyme, and stir. Heat until all the ingredients are well combined.

Add a dash of Tabasco sauce, salt and pepper to taste.

Remove from heat, cool and serve.

Recipe video tutorial

https://youtu.be/8T7s6w1sYqQ

MANGO SALSA

Makes 4 to 6 servings

Ingredients:

1/4 cup cilantro chopped

Juice of 1 lime

1 jalapeño pepper diced

1/2 cup or 75g red bell pepper diced

1/2 cup or 75g orange bell pepper diced

1 red onion or 85g diced

1 cup or 190g pineapple diced

1/2 cup or 110g tomatoes diced

1 cup or 190g mango diced

1/4 cup or 77g sweet chili sauce

2 tbsp or 30ml extra virgin olive oil

1/2 tsp salt

Chop the cilantro and dice the jalapeño (remove the center membrane and seeds if you don't like it hot), red and orange bell peppers, onion, pineapple, tomatoes, mango (use a potato peeler to remove the skin, cut around the center pit to remove the mango flesh, and finally dice the mango flesh into bite-size pieces).

Add all the chopped/diced ingredients, juice of one lime, sweet chili sauce, and salt to a glass bowl. Mix well.

Have it on the spot or cover it and put it in the fridge for at least an hour to marry the flavors.

Recipe video tutorial

https://youtu.be/TyWF7xrZ-e4

CHIVE SAUCE

Makes 1 cup or 250ml

Add all the ingredients to a bowl, mix and you're ready to serve.

Ingredients:

1/2 cup or 125g sour cream

1/4 cup or 63ml mayonnaise

1 tsp Dijon mustard

2 tbsp finally chopped chives

2 tbsp or 30g honey

2 tbsp or 30ml lemon Juice

Salt and pepper to taste

Recipe video tutorial

https://youtu.be/e97mFbgNpOc

PARSLEY LEMON SAUCE

Makes 1/2 cup or 125ml

Ingredients:

White fish of your choice

1/4 cup or 63ml white wine (ex: Chardonnay)

3/4 cup or 187ml heavy cream

Zest of half a lemon

1 tbsp or 15ml lemon juice

2 tbsp parsley chopped

Pinch of pepper

Dash of salt

Fry the fish in a pan using the neutral oil. Remove the fish and put it in a warm place. Make sure to leave any bits and pieces of the fish on the bottom of the pan – this will add flavor to the sauce.

Deglaze the pan by adding the white wine to the pan over medium heat. Use a spatula or spoon to scrape the sides and bottom of the pan to add the bits and pieces of fish up into the liquid. Reduce the wine until there is roughly 1 tbsp or 15ml left in the pan.

Pour in the heavy cream and add the lemon juice and zest. Stir and simmer over medium heat to reduce until thick (the sauce will coat the back of a spoon).

Take the sauce off heat. Add the chopped parsley and stir.

Add salt and pepper to taste.

Recipe video tutorial

https://youtu.be/9v8Wr4G_xYA

TARRAGON AND TOMATO SAUCE

Makes 3/4 cup or 187ml

Ingredients:

White fish of your choice

5 tbsp or 70g unsalted butter

1 chopped shallot

1/2 tsp chopped tarragon

1/2 cup or 125ml white wine (ex: Chardonnay)

Dash of black pepper

1 medium tomato diced

Pan fry the fish of your choice (white meat fish are best).

Remove the fish from the pan and melt 1 tbsp or 14g butter over medium heat.

Add the shallots, cook until tender.

Add the tarragon and deglaze the pan with the white wine. Reduce the wine by 3/4th over medium heat and scrape the bottom of the pan to mix the bits and pieces of fish into the liquid.

Crack in a touch of black pepper, add the diced tomato, and simmer on low heat until thick (2 to 5 minutes).

Remove the sauce from heat, add 4 tbsp or 56g of cubed cold butter. Use a spoon to stir the butter into the sauce or you can swirl the sauce in the pan to mix it in.

Taste and add additional salt or pepper as needed.

Recipe video tutorial

https://youtu.be/NVpQS_leuRA

barbecues into a culinary celebration of smoky perfection under the vast, open sky.

BBQ SAUCES AND GLAZES

Step into the smoky and flavorful ambiance of BBQ Sauces and Glazes, where the tantalizing aroma of grilling and the great outdoors converge. In this chapter, immerse yourself in the art of enhancing your outdoor barbecue experience with an array of mouthwatering sauces and glazes. From the tangy sweetness of a classic Kansas City barbecue sauce to the spicy kick of a smoky cherry chipotle glaze, these recipes are tailored to elevate your grilled masterpieces amidst the fresh air and open skies. Whether you fancy a traditional Southern-style barbecue sauce or a honey-soy glaze with an outdoor-inspired Asian twist, this collection caters to every barbecue enthusiast's palate. Delve into the exciting world of BBQ sauces and glazes, where each brushstroke adds depth and character to your favorite grilled dishes. Get ready to unleash a symphony of flavors and turn your outdoor

ASIAN-STYLE BBQ SAUCE

Makes 3/4 cup or 187ml

Ingredients:

6 tbsp or 90ml hoisin sauce

2 tbsp or 30ml rice vinegar

1 tbsp or 15ml Asian fish sauce

1 tbsp or 15ml soy sauce

1 tbsp or 15g honey

1/3 cup or 55g shallots minced

1 tbsp or 12g fresh ginger peeled and minced

2 garlic cloves minced

1/3 cup or 60g brown sugar

1/8 tsp five spice

In a mixing bowl, combine the hoisin sauce, rice vinegar, fish sauce, soy sauce, honey, minced shallots, garlic and ginger. Mix well.

Add the brown sugar to a separate saucepot, then turn the burner on low to medium heat and slowly melt. When the sugar is fully melted, stir in the ingredients from the mixing bowl. Gently simmer for 2 minutes.

Mix in the five spice and continue to simmer for 3 to 6 more minutes or until thick.

Tip:

The mixture may spit and bubble so be careful not to burn yourself.

If the sugar turns into a hard ball, keep stirring and it will eventually dissolve in the liquid.

Recipe video tutorial

https://youtu.be/Ax4-AQVlSV0

BLUEBERRY CHIPOTLE BBQ SAUCE

Makes about 1 cup or 250ml

Ingredients:

1 cup or 150g fresh blueberries

1/2 cup or 125g ketchup

1/2 cup or 125ml apple cider vinegar

1 clove of garlic

1.5 tsp chipotle chili powder

1 tbsp or 15g brown sugar

1 tbsp or 15ml maple syrup

To a saucepan, add all the ingredients except the maple syrup and stir. Then turn the burner on to medium heat. Mix well, bring to a simmer and slowly reduce for 10 to 15 minutes.

Add the maple syrup, stir and heat for 1 minute.

Transfer the sauce to a blender and blend until smooth.

Recipe video tutorial

https://youtu.be/bFo8QEsbM5c

CAROLINA GOLD
BBQ SAUCE

Makes 2 cups or 500ml

Ingredients:

1 cup or 230g yellow mustard

1/4 cup or 57g light brown sugar

1 tbsp or 15g ketchup

1 tbsp or 22g diced chipotle peppers in adobo
sauce

1/4 cup or 75g honey

1 tsp garlic powder

Dash of black pepper to taste

1/2 cup or 125ml apple cider vinegar

2 tsp Worcestershire sauce

Add all the ingredients to a mixing bowl, stir, and
you're ready to serve.

Tips:

Using a whisk helps make a smooth sauce.

For a full flavor experience, let the sauce sit
covered in the fridge overnight.

Recipe video tutorial

https://youtu.be/K0aB29A8Xyl

CHERRY CHIPOTLE BBQ SAUCE

Makes 1 ½ cups or 375ml

Ingredients:

1/2 cup or 125g ketchup

1 tbsp molasses (unsulfured)

1/2 cup or 125ml red wine vinegar

1/4 tsp garlic powder

1/4 tsp black pepper

1/4 tsp paprika

1/4 tsp allspice

1/8 tsp cayenne pepper

1.5 tsp chipotle chili powder

1 tsp hickory-flavored liquid smoke

1 cup or 150g cherries

Salt to taste

Add the ketchup, molasses, red wine vinegar, garlic powder, black pepper, paprika, all spice, cayenne pepper, chipotle chili powder, and liquid smoke to a saucepot. Mix and then turn the heat to medium.

Add the cherries, stir and bring to a simmer. Then turn the heat to low and reduce for roughly 20 minutes or by half.

Taste the sauce and season with salt and additional pepper or spices as needed.

Blend the sauce in a blender and you're ready to hit the grill.

Recipe video tutorial

https://youtu.be/3p4ZYxNKOQE

HAWAIIAN PINEAPPLE BBQ SAUCE

Makes 2 ½ cups or 625ml

Ingredients:

1 cup or 200g chopped pineapple

3/4 cup or 160g light brown sugar

1/2 cup or 125g ketchup

1 clove of garlic

2 tbsp or 30ml soy sauce

3 tbsp or 45ml rice vinegar

2 tbsp or 30ml Worcestershire sauce

1/4 tsp cayenne pepper

1 tsp ground ginger

1 tbsp arrowroot

Combine all ingredients in a blender and blend until smooth.

Pour the sauce into a saucepan. Bring to a simmer over medium heat to infuse the flavors and activate the arrowroot that will thicken the sauce.

Taste the sauce and adjust the seasoning as needed.

Tip:

The arrowroot can be substituted with cornstarch.

Recipe video tutorial

https://youtu.be/57NCzNmsPVw

HICKORY SMOKE TERIYAKI SAUCE

Makes 1 cup or 250ml

Ingredients:

1/3 cup or 83ml sake

1/3 cup or 83ml mirin

1/3 cup or 83ml low sodium soy sauce

1/2 tsp hickory-flavored liquid smoke

1/2 cup or 91g light brown sugar

2 tbsp or 40g ground ginger

2 tbsp or 15g cornstarch

2 tbsp or 30ml water

Make a cornstarch slurry: To a small bowl, add 2 tbsp or 30ml water to 2 tbsp or 15g cornstarch. Mix and set to the side.

To make the sauce:

Pour the sake, mirin, soy sauce, hickory-flavored liquid smoke and add the light brown sugar and ground ginger to a saucepan. Then turn the burner up to medium heat, stir and bring to a simmer for 1 minute.

Give the cornstarch slurry a quick stir and slowly pour it into the sauce while whisking.

Bring the sauce back to a simmer.

Remove the sauce from heat once it starts to thicken up and you're ready to dive in.

Recipe video tutorial

https://youtu.be/a-DNGqeNWRI

KC-STYLE BBQ SAUCE

Makes 1 cup or 250ml

Ingredients:

1/2 cup or 125g ketchup

1/2 cup or 125g tomato sauce

1/3 cup or 83ml red wine vinegar

1/8 cup or 32ml molasses (unsulfured)

1/3 cup or 63g dark brown sugar

1/8 tsp onion powder

1/8 tsp garlic powder

Pinch of chili powder

Dash of allspice

1/4 tsp smoked paprika

1/8 tsp cayenne pepper

1/8 tsp celery seed

1/4 tsp pepper

1/8 tsp salt

1 tsp hickory-flavored liquid smoke

1/2 tbsp or 7g unsalted butter

Combine all the ingredients except the butter in a saucepot, mix, and turn the heat to medium. Bring to a light simmer, then lower the heat. Reduce for 20 minutes or until the sauce is thick.

Turn off the heat and stir in the butter. Then enjoy!

Recipe video tutorial

https://youtu.be/WvhdTlUykXU

SWEET AND SPICY SAUCE OR GLAZE

Makes 3/4 cup or 187ml

Ingredients:

1/2 cup or 125ml rice vinegar

1 cup or 200g light brown sugar

3 tsp red pepper flakes

2 cloves of garlic minced

Add all the ingredients to a saucepot. Mix well. Then turn the burner on medium heat. Once the sauce starts to simmer, turn the heat to low and cook for 8 to 10 minutes until thick.

Take the sauce off heat when it is thick as syrup.

Recipe video tutorial

https://youtu.be/7u-nX1NjErs

SWEET AND SPICY BARBECUE SAUCE

Makes 1 1/3 cups or 333ml

Ingredients:

1/2 jalapeno pepper diced

1/4 cup or 33g onion finely

1 clove of garlic minced

1/4 tsp celery seed

1/4 tsp red pepper flakes

1/2 tbsp or 7ml neutral oil

1/2 cup or 125g tomato sauce

1/2 cup or 125g ketchup

1/4 cup or 55g dark brown sugar

1/8 cup or 32ml apple juice

1/8 cup or 35g honey

1/2 tbsp or 7ml Worcestershire sauce

1/4 tsp black pepper

1/4 tsp salt

1/4 tsp cayenne pepper

1/4 cup or 63ml apple cider vinegar

Slice the jalapeno in half, remove the internal white membrane and seeds (if you like it hot, don't remove the membrane or seeds), and dice into small pieces.

Finely mince the onion and the garlic.

Add red pepper flakes, celery seeds, and salt to a mortar and crush them with the pestle until they form a fine powder - you can use a coffee grinder if you don't have a mortar and pestle (grinding is optional).

To a saucepan over medium heat, add the neutral oil. Heat and add the minced onion and garlic. Cook until tender and soft.

Pour in the ketchup, tomato sauce, brown sugar, apple juice, spices (red pepper flakes, celery seeds and salt), honey, Worcestershire Sauce, apple cider vinegar, cayenne pepper and black pepper into the saucepan. Stir, bring to a simmer over medium heat, then turn the heat down and slowly simmer on low for 25 minutes.

 Tip:

If you want a smooth sauce – add the sauce to a blender and blend until smooth.

Recipe video tutorial

https://youtu.be/DUpKXeZhLyY

COMFORT FOODS

In the cozy kitchen of uplifting indulgence, gather around the heartwarming hearth of Comfort Foods. This chapter warmly welcomes you to explore the nostalgic and soul-soothing haven of dishes that go beyond mere sustenance, invoking feelings of warmth, joy, and a sense of home. From the timeless charm of classic sloppy Joes, reminiscent of childhood simplicity, to the heartiness of loaded chicken alfredo casserole that wraps you in comfort on chilly evenings, these recipes are more than just nourishment—they're a celebration of the deep connection between food and cherished emotions. Whether it's the inviting aroma of freshly baked buttermilk biscuits and gravy or the familiar flavors of a treasured family recipe, comfort foods possess a unique magic, weaving memories both old and new. Savor the simple, homely pleasures that come with each comforting bite, as you navigate through a collection that pays tribute to the enduring charm of comforting flavors found in the heart of your kitchen.

BUTTERMILK BISCUITS AND GRAVY

Gravy: Makes 3 cups or 750ml

Biscuits: Makes eighteen 2" biscuits

Ingredients:

Buttermilk Biscuits

2.5 cups or 395g self-rising flour

2 tbsp or 22g granulated white sugar

1/2 cup or 114.5g unsalted butter frozen

1 cup or 250ml buttermilk

Sausage Gravy

1 lb. or 500g breakfast sausage

3 tbsp or 24g all-purpose flour

3 cups or 750ml milk

Cracked black pepper to your taste

Salt to your taste

To make the biscuits:

Add the self-rising flour and sugar to a bowl and give it a mix. Take the butter out of the freezer and shred it in a food processor, then add it to the bowl with the flour – try not to touch the butter with your hands. Mix lightly until combined. Make a well in the center of the flour mixture, pour the buttermilk in, and gently mix to incorporate the liquid.

Transfer the dough to a well-floured work surface. Knead and shape it into a square or rectangle. Fold it in half and roll it out to roughly 1 inch thick. Turn the dough clockwise and repeat the folding/rolling process roughly 4 to 7 times. On the last fold, shape the dough into a rectangle or square 3/4 inch thick.

Use a biscuit cutter or floured mason jar to punch out the biscuits. Closely place the biscuits on a parchment lined baking sheet. Roundup any leftover dough, shape and roll it out and repeat the process until all the dough has been used.

Brush the tops of the biscuits with buttermilk. Bake them in a pre-heated oven at 450° F or 232° C for 15 to 20 minutes until cooked through and lightly browned.

To make the sausage gravy:

Place the ground sausage in a cold skillet. Turn the burner to medium-high heat. Use a flat bottom spatula to break up the sausage into small pieces and cook through.

Sprinkle the flour on the sausage, stir and cook on medium for 2 to 3 minutes. Pour in milk, mix well scraping the sides and bottom of the pan. Add black pepper, stir frequently and bring to a simmer. Cook until the gravy is as thick as you like.

Give the gravy a taste and adjust the seasoning. Add salt or additional pepper if needed.

Recipe video tutorial

https://youtu.be/2lJAgsPFF6A

To plate the dish:

Open the biscuits by breaking them in half. Place them with the inside of the biscuits facing up. Add the gravy over the top and enjoy.

CREAMY ALFREDO SAUCE

Makes 4 to 6 servings

Ingredients:

4 tbsp or 56g unsalted butter

3 cloves garlic minced

1.5 cups or 375ml heavy cream

1.5 cups or 80g grated parmesan Reggiano

1/4 tsp white pepper

Dash of salt

10oz or 235g fettuccine (dry)

To a high sided saucepan over low to medium heat, add butter and gently melt it down.

Add the minced garlic, simmer for 2 to 3 minutes to gradually infuse its flavor.

Pour in the heavy cream, heat on low for 3 to 5 minutes without simmering.

Once the mixture starts to steam, add the parmesan cheese in batches.   Heat on low for 3 to 5 minutes, frequently stirring.

When the sauce becomes thick and coats the back of a spoon, add a dash of white pepper.

Give the sauce a taste and add salt if needed. If you would like to add additional ingredients like cooked chicken or broccoli, it can be added now.

Add the cooked fettuccine to the sauce and enjoy.

Recipe video tutorial

https://youtu.be/ncYKqz-TcNQ

CHICKEN ALFREDO CASSEROLE

6 tbsp or 48g all-purpose flour

2 cups or 500ml chicken stock

2 cups or 500ml heavy cream

Dash of black pepper and salt

3 cups or 330g mozzarella

Makes 6 to 8 servings

Ingredients:

3 chicken breasts or 3 cups shredded chicken (fully cooked)

16oz penne pasta (dry)

2 cups or broccoli

1 cup or 63g grated parmesan

2 tbsp chopped oregano

2 tbsp chopped basil – stems saved

2 tbsp flat leaf parsley chopped– stems saved

Fresh or dried thyme sprigs

1 cup or 130g diced red onion

6 slices or 210g bacon chopped

2 tbsp or 30ml neutral oil

3 large handfuls of spinach

5 minced cloves of garlic

1/4 cup or 63ml dry white wine

1/4 tsp red pepper flakes

5 tbsp or 70g unsalted butter

Poach the chicken. Cook it completely. Prepare the pasta in salted water per the manufacturer's instructions. Boil or steam the broccoli. Finely chop the oregano, basil, and parsley leaves– save the parsley and basil stems. Dice the red onion and cut the bacon into bite-size pieces.

To make the sauce:

Add the oil to a high-sided saucepan over medium to high heat and add the spinach. Sauté until tender and remove from the pan. Add bacon to the pan and completely cook over medium heat. Then add the red onion and cook until tender.

Add the garlic and sauté for roughly 30 seconds. Pour in the white wine, add red pepper flakes, a pinch of oregano, basil and parsley. Reduce the wine until it is nearly all gone.

Make a well in the center of the pan and add 5 tbsp or 70g of butter. Melt, add the flour, stir and cook for 2 minutes over medium heat.

Add the chicken stock, heavy cream, a touch of black pepper, and stir. Add the parsley and basil stems, cook over medium heat for roughly 5 minutes or until thick.

Take the sauce off heat and remove the stems. Add the parmesan cheese and mix. Then add 1 cup or 110g mozzarella. Stir until smooth. Add the spinach back in the sauce, with another pinch of oregano, basil, and parsley. Combine well.

To make the casserole:

Drain the pasta and broccoli. Shred the chicken.

Combine the pasta, broccoli, chicken and sauce in a Dutch oven or baking dish. Give all the ingredients a good mix and top with 2 cups or 220g mozzarella.

Bake in a pre-heated oven at 375˚ F or 190˚ C for 20 to 25 minutes or until the cheese is bubbly and lightly golden brown on the top.

Recipe video tutorial

https://youtu.be/OhLRkZABJOQ

WHITE GRAVY FOR CHICKEN FRIED STEAK

Makes 4 to 6 servings

Ingredients:

4 to 6 cube steaks

Neutral oil to fry the steaks – 1.5in or 3.8cm deep in the pan

Dredging Liquid

1.5 cups or 375ml milk

1 tbsp or 15ml apple cider vinegar

1 tbsp 15ml Tabasco sauce

2 eggs

Dredging Flour Mixture

1.5 cups or 230g all-purpose flour

1/2 tsp of each: paprika, onion powder, garlic powder, black pepper, and salt

White Gravy

4 tbsp or 50g of the dredging flour mixture

4 tbsp or 60ml neutral oil

3 cups or 750ml milk

1/2 cup or 125ml heavy cream

Pepper and salt taste

To make the chicken fried steaks:

Place all the dredging liquid ingredients in a deep dish or bowl, and mix. Add all the cube steaks to the liquid, cover and let rest in the fridge for at least an hour.

Add all the dredging flour ingredients to another deep dish or bowl. Mix well. Scoop out and reserve 4 tbsp or 32g of the dredging flour mixture and place it to the side (it will be used later to make the gravy).

Once rested, take each individual steak out of the dredging liquid, remove any excess liquid, and place it in the dredging flour mixture to coat it. Optional: double dredge the steaks by repeating the process. Once well-coated, set to the side.

To a large saucepan, add a generous amount of neutral oil – deep enough to cover the steaks. Fry the steaks in batches over medium to high heat, about 2 to 3 minutes per side or until cooked through and golden brown. Remove and place on a wire rack.

When you're done frying the steaks, take 4 tbsp or 75ml of the cooking oil in which you fried the steaks, and put it to the side to make the gravy.

To make the gravy:

To a saucepan over medium heat, add the reserved 4 tbsp cooking oil used to fry the steak, and 4 tbsp dredging flour you put to the side and mix. Cook for 2 to 3 minutes. The mixture should look like wet sand – add more oil or butter if needed.

Pour in the milk, stir, and add black pepper. Bring to a simmer, cook until thick, and add heavy cream. Mix and cook for 2 to 5 minutes or until thick.

Taste and add salt and additional pepper as needed.

Recipe video tutorial

https://youtu.be/KEq2DPzuG3s

HAMBURGER GRAVY

Makes 4 to 6 servings

Ingredients:

1 tbsp or 14g unsalted butter

1 tbsp or 15ml neutral oil

1 lb. or 500g ground beef

1/2 cup or 63g onions chopped

3 tbsp or 32g all-purpose flour

1 tsp beef bouillon

1 cup or 250ml milk

1 cup or 250ml heavy cream

1 tbsp Worcestershire Sauce

1 tsp soy sauce

Add butter and oil to a high-sided saucepan over medium to high heat and melt. Add the ground beef. Use a flat bottom spatula to break the ground beef into small pieces and cook until there is just a hint of redness left in the meat.

Add the onions, stir, and cook until they are tender and the meat is fully cooked.

Sprinkle the flour over the beef, stir, and cook over low to medium heat for 2 minutes.

Pour in the milk, then the heavy cream and stir. Add the beef bouillon, Worcestershire sauce and soy sauce. Bring to a simmer over medium heat, stir, and cook until thick.

Taste and add salt and pepper to taste.

Recipe video tutorial

https://youtu.be/XnK1_SkWkgk

SOS GRAVY
CHIPPED BEEF GRAVY

Makes 4 to 6 servings

Ingredients:

4 tbsp or 56g unsalted butter

2.25oz or 64g dried beef

4 tbsp or 32g all-purpose flour

2 cups or 500ml milk

1/2 tsp black pepper

Dash of cayenne pepper

Dash of salt (optional)

Cut the dried beef into small strips or chips.

Add butter to a skillet over medium to high heat and melt it down.

Drop in the dried beef and sauté for 30 seconds. Sprinkle the flour onto the beef, stir and cook for 2 to 3 minutes.

Pour in the milk, stir and cook over medium heat. Once the sauce starts to simmer, turn the heat to low, and add the black pepper and cayenne pepper. Cook until the gravy is as thick as desired.

Tips:

To reduce the sodium level, wash the dried beef in water before you cut it up.

Recipe video tutorial

https://youtu.be/vOw9DrWx0Tc

LOADED SALISBURY STEAKS

Makes 4 to 6 servings

Ingredients:

Hamburger Steak

1 lb. or 500g ground beef

1/4 cup or 35g bread crumbs

1 packet of onion soup mix

1/2 tsp ground mustard

1 large egg

2 tbsp or 30ml Worcestershire sauce

1 to 2 tbsp or 15 to 30ml neutral oil

Mushroom and Onion Gravy

5 tbsp or 70g unsalted butter

1 medium onion or 150g

2.5 cups or 227g sliced mushrooms (one 8oz box)

2 garlic cloves minced

1/3 cup or 83ml red wine

3 cups or 750ml beef broth

1 tbsp or 15ml Worcestershire sauce

1 tsp of low sodium soy sauce

3 tbsp or 55g ketchup

Salt and pepper to taste

To make the Salisbury steaks:

Add all the hamburger steak ingredients to a bowl, mix, cover, and let the meat rest in the refrigerator for at least an hour. Then pat out four 1/4 pound or 125g Salisbury steak patties.

Pour the oil into a high-sided saucepan over medium to high heat. Add the Steaks, sear the steaks for 2 minutes on each side to give color (they will be cooked through later with the gravy), remove them, cover and put to the side.

To make the gravy:

Add 2 tbsp or 28g butter to the same pan the steaks were cooked in. Melt it down over medium heat. Once hot, add the onions and mushrooms, sauté until tender and slightly brown. At the tail end of cooking this mixture, add the minced garlic and cook for 30 seconds.

Pour red wine into the pan, stir, and reduce it down until it's nearly all gone.

Make a well in the center of the pan. Add 3 tbsp or 42g butter and melt. Mix the flour into the melted butter, then combine with all the ingredients and cook for 2 to 3 minutes.

Add beef broth, Worcestershire sauce, soy sauce, and ketchup. Mix and bring to a simmer over medium heat. Then add the steaks back into the pan and cook for 10 to 25 minutes until the steaks are done and the gravy is thick.

Taste the gravy, adjust the seasoning with salt and pepper if needed and enjoy!

Recipe video tutorial

https://youtu.be/D5lFQHKw1tc

SOUTHWEST CHICKEN SPAGHETTI

Makes 6 to 8 servings

Ingredients:

3 cups shredded chicken (3 chicken breasts)

12oz to 16oz spaghetti (dry)

1 lb. or 450g cheddar cheese

1 red bell pepper

1 green bell pepper

1 medium white onion

2 tbsp or 30ml neutral oil

6 tbsp or 90g bacon grease

6 tbsp or 48g all-purpose flour

2 cups or 500ml chicken broth or stock

2 cups or 500ml heavy cream

One 10oz can diced tomatoes and green chilis

One 15oz can of corn - drained

2 tsp oregano

2 tsp cumin

2 tsp chili powder

Pinch of cayenne pepper

1/2 tsp onion powder

Prep work:

Poach the chicken for at least 15 minutes or until done, shred or chop it into bite-size pieces (you can also use canned or rotisserie chicken). Cook the spaghetti per the manufacturer's instructions. Grate the cheddar cheese. Chop the red and green bell peppers, as well as the onion.

To make the sauce:

Add oil into a high-sided saucepan over high heat. Add the onion and the red and green bell peppers. Stir and cook until they are lightly golden brown. Make a well in the center of the pan and add the bacon grease, melt it and mix in the flour. Then combine with the vegetables and cook for 2 to 3 minutes. Add the chicken broth and stir. Then pour in the heavy cream, bring to a simmer, reduce the heat to low and cook for 5 minutes.

Add the diced tomatoes and green chilis, corn, oregano, cumin, cayenne pepper, chili powder and onion powder. Bring to a simmer on low for 5 to 10 minutes or until thick.

Take the sauce off heat and add 2 cups or 225g shredded cheddar cheese in batches. Taste the sauce to see if the seasoning needs to be adjusted.

Add salt, pepper or additional herbs and spices as needed.

To prepare the baked pasta:

To a Dutch oven or 9 x 13" baking dish, add in layers the sauce, the chicken, and the pasta. Mix well then top with 2 cups or 225g of shredded cheddar cheese.

Baking instructions:

Place in a pre-heated oven at 350˚F or 176˚C for 50 to 60 minutes (in Dutch oven). If using a 9 x 13" baking dish, check after 30 to 40 minutes to see if it's done.

When it is bubbly and the cheese is lightly golden brown, it's ready to be taken out of the oven.

Recipe video tutorial

https://youtu.be/ZvDDRB5sKq8

SLOPPY JOES

Makes 4 to 6 servings

Ingredients:

2 tbsp or 30g bacon grease

1 medium yellow onion diced

1 medium green bell pepper diced

2 garlic cloves minced

1 lb. or 500g ground beef 93% lean

1/4 cup or 63ml Madeira wine

15oz can tomato sauce

1.5 tbsp or 35g yellow mustard

1 tbsp or 15g dark brown sugar

1/2 tsp red pepper flakes

1/2 tbsp or 7ml soy sauce

1 tbsp or 15ml Worcestershire sauce

1 cup or 250ml chicken broth or stock

Salt and pepper to taste

Melt the bacon grease in a large saucepan over medium to high heat, add the onion and bell pepper, and cook until tender.

Make a well in the center of the pan and add the ground beef, break it up into small pieces with a flat-bottom spatula. Combine with peppers and onions and cook until done.

Add minced garlic and cook for 30 seconds.

Pour in the Madeira wine to deglaze the pan, and reduce it until it's nearly all gone.

Add the tomato sauce, dark brown sugar, red pepper flakes, yellow mustard, soy sauce, Worcestershire sauce, chicken broth, and a touch of salt. Bring to a simmer over medium heat. Then turn the heat to low and reduce for 20 to 25 minutes or until the sauce becomes thick.

Once the sauce's liquid is pretty much all gone and you can scoop the sloppy joe onto a spatula and it stays stacked high, you are ready to make a mess and enjoy!

Tip:

Use a lean ground beef. That way, your Sloppy Joes will be deliciously messy, but not greasy.

Recipe video tutorial

https://youtu.be/Ylm4IeXKn4Y

SWEDISH MEATBALLS

Makes 4 to 6 servings

Ingredients:

Meatballs

1 lb. or 500g ground beef (or ½ lb. ground beef and ½ lb. ground pork)

1 tbsp parsley chopped

1/4 cup or 33g bread crumbs

1/4 tsp each: allspice, nutmeg, garlic powder

1/4 cup or 30g onion chopped

1 egg

Salt and pepper to taste

Neutral Oil – enough to fry the meatballs

Sauce

5 tbsp or 70g unsalted butter

3 tbsp or 24g all-purpose flour

2 cups or 500ml beef or brown veal stock

2 tbsp or 30ml Worcestershire sauce

1/2 tbsp or 7ml soy sauce

1 cup or 250ml heavy cream

1/4 tsp mustard powder

Salt and pepper to taste

2 tbsp parsley chopped (to garnish)

To make the meatballs:

Add all the meatball ingredients to a bowl, mix with your hands or a spatula. Optional: you may sauté the onions and fresh minced garlic and also soak the bread crumbs in 1/8 cup of cream.

Pat the meat into balls – the size of golf balls.

Fry the meatballs in a pan with neutral oil until golden brown and cooked through. Remove them from the pan.

To make the sauce:

Remove the grease from the pan, but leave all the bits and pieces. Add the butter and melt over medium heat. Then add flour, mix and scrape the bottom of the pan to release the bits and pieces of meatballs. Cook for 2 minutes.

Add the stock. Use a flat-bottom spatula to scrape the bottom of the pan. Then add the Worcestershire sauce, soy sauce, heavy cream, and mustard powder. Stir, bring to a simmer over medium heat, and cook until the sauce coats the back of a spoon.

Taste and adjust the seasoning with salt and pepper if needed. You're ready to serve the sauce alongside the meatballs, mashed potatoes and Lingonberries.

Recipe video tutorial

https://youtu.be/XAm9Kbv03xw

HOLIDAY SAUCES

In the heartwarming embrace of Holiday Sauces and Gravies, the magic of the season unfolds in every family-inspired creation. Gathering around the holiday table, this collection extends a cozy invitation to revel in the cherished joy of celebration through an array of sauces and gravies that bring a true family feel to your festive feasts. Picture the velvety richness of a decadent fruity cranberry sauce or the comforting hug of a perfectly seasoned turkey gravy, elevating the homely flavors of your holiday favorites. Whether aiming to add a touch of holiday charm with a full-flavored drippings gravy or seeking the heartwarming sweetness of a spiced applesauce, these sauces and gravies are thoughtfully crafted to transform your holiday meals into moments of shared joy and love. Take a culinary journey and explore the art of saucing during this special time of the year. Get ready to infuse your holiday gatherings with the comforting familiarity of flavor, as you dive into the heartwarming world of holiday sauces and gravies, capturing the true essence of joyous family occasions.

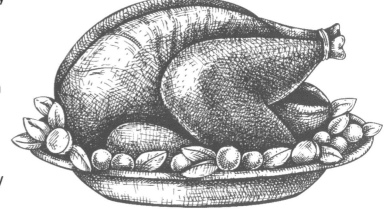

CREAMY MUSTARD HORSERADISH SAUCE

Add all the ingredients to a mixing bowl and stir.

Makes 1 ½ cups or 375ml

Recipe video tutorial

https://youtu.be/OlTbfljTCm4

Ingredients:

1/2 cup or 125ml mayonnaise

1 cup or 250g sour cream

3 tbsp prepared horseradish

2 tsp Dijon mustard

2 sprigs of fresh dill chopped

2 tsp white wine vinegar

1/4 tsp salt

AU JUS

Makes 1 ½ cups or 375ml

Ingredients:

Roasting Pan

Rib roast

Handful of parsley and rosemary

1/2 onion chopped or 110g

2 carrots diced or 150g

2 celery sticks/stems chopped or 113g

4 cloves of garlic

Sauce

1/2 cup or 125ml red wine

1.5 cups or 375ml brown veal stock or brown stock

1 tbsp or 15ml Worcestershire sauce

When cooking the roast, add herbs and aromatics to the bottom of the roasting pan and place the roast on top. Once the roast is cooked, remove it from the pan, leaving the aromatics. Put the roasting pan over a burner on low heat, add red wine, and use a flat-bottom spatula to scrape the bottom of the pan. Reduce the wine until almost gone.

Add veal stock and Worcestershire sauce. Turn the burner up to medium heat, stir and heat for 2 to 5 minutes.

Strain the cooking liquid into a gravy boat or bowl and enjoy!

Recipe video tutorial

https://youtu.be/OlTbfljTCm4

SPICY HORSERADISH SAUCE

Makes 1 cup or 250ml

Ingredients:

3/4 cup or 188g sour cream

2 tbsp or 30ml mayonnaise

4 tbsp freshly ground horseradish

Dash of Worcestershire sauce

1/2 tsp white wine vinegar

1 tbsp green onion chopped (green part of the onion)

Dash of salt and black pepper

Add all the ingredients to a mixing bowl and stir.

Recipe video tutorial

https://youtu.be/OlTbfljTCm4

APPLESAUCE

Makes 4 to 6 Servings

Ingredients:

3 lbs. apples (5 to 7 medium apples of any kind)

1/4 cup or 52g granulated white sugar (optional)

1/2 tsp cinnamon (optional)

1/4 tsp salt

2 tbsp or 30ml lemon juice

1/2 cup or 125ml water

Core, peel, and dice the apples.

To a saucepan over medium to medium-high heat, add the apples, sugar, cinnamon, salt, lemon juice, and water. Stir, bring to a simmer, then reduce heat to low and cook covered for 15 to 20 minutes.

Once the apples are tender/cooked, blend the sauce until it is as smooth or as chunky as you like.

Recipe video tutorial

https://youtu.be/xrsn_8vjt4g

PEAR SAUCE

Recipe video tutorial

https://youtu.be/Gf5O2noAN8A

Makes 4 to 6 Servings

Ingredients:

5 cups or 780g cored, peeled, and diced pears (3 to 4 pears)

1/4 cup or 63ml water

1 tsp vanilla extract

2 tsp lemon juice

1/4 cup or 52g granulated white sugar

1/2 tsp ground ginger

1 tbsp or 15ml orange liquor

1/2 tsp ground cinnamon

Zest of 1 lemon

Add all the ingredients to a saucepan. Stir well.

Bring to a simmer over medium heat. Then reduce heat to low and cook for 20 to 25 minutes or until the pears are tender.

Blend until smooth.

CAJUN-STYLE COCKTAIL SAUCE

Makes 1 cup or 250ml

Ingredients:

3/4 cup or 188g ketchup

1/4 cup or 63ml chili sauce (ex: Sriracha chili sauce)

1/4 tsp garlic powder

1/4 tsp onion powder

1 tbsp ground horseradish

1/2 tbsp lemon juice

1 tsp Worcestershire sauce

Dash of Tabasco sauce

Salt and pepper to taste

Add all the ingredients to a bowl and mix well.

Recipe video tutorial

https://youtu.be/KA0-39H9NOo

CLASSIC RED SHRIMP COCKTAIL SAUCE

Makes 1 cup or 250ml

Ingredients:

1 cup or 250g ketchup

1 tbsp ground horseradish

1 lemon juiced

1 tsp Worcestershire sauce

Dash of Tabasco sauce

Add all the ingredients to a bowl and mix well.

Recipe video tutorial

https://youtu.be/aJx8SqkmlVQ

DUCK à L'ORANGE

Makes 3/4 cup or 188ml

Ingredients:

4 to 6 duck breasts

3 oranges zested and juiced

1 lemon zested

3 tbsp or 45g granulated white sugar

1/3 cup or 83ml red wine vinegar

2 cups or 500ml brown veal stock or brown stock

2 tbsp or 30ml orange liqueur

Add water to a saucepan and bring it to a rolling boil. Then add the zest of three oranges and one lemon and simmer for 5 minutes. Strain and place the zests in an icy water bath and set to the side.

Juice three oranges (you will need 1 cup or 250ml orange juice).

To make the gastrique:

Add sugar and red wine vinegar to a saucepan. Bring to a simmer and cook until it becomes a thick syrupy amber color.

Pour in your orange juice, stir and bring back to a simmer over medium heat.

Once the sugar and vinegar mixture has dissolved and is well combined with the orange juice, add the brown stock. Return to a simmer over medium heat. Skim the foam/impurities off the top while the sauce reduces down by half. Put to the side.

To cook the duck breast:

Score the fat side of the duck with a knife (a nice checker pattern works well). Dry each breast with a paper towel and season with salt and pepper. Place the duck breast fat side down into a sauté pan, then turn the heat to medium and cook for 6 to 8 minutes. Turn the breast over and cook for another 3 to 4 minutes until cooked to your liking or until the internal temperature reaches 165° F or 74° C (Per USDA).

Remove the breast and duck fat from the pan, but keep all the bits and pieces of duck that are encrusted on the bottom of the pan.

Add the previously made gastrique and brown sauce combo to the pan. Turn the heat to medium. Take a flat-bottom spatula and scrape the sides and bottom of the pan to release the fond into the sauce. Bring the sauce to a light simmer and cook

For 5 to 8 minutes or until the sauce is reduced by half or is as thick as you would like.

Take the sauce off heat and strain it into a clean saucepan. Add the orange liqueur and the orange and lemon zests, and simmer for a minute.

Taste and adjust the seasoning – add salt and pepper as needed.

Recipe video tutorial

https://youtu.be/nOeDls_zbuU

TURKEY GIBLET GRAVY

Makes 2 cups or 500ml

Ingredients:

Giblet Stock

Giblets: heart, gizzard, neck and liver

3 sprigs of parsley

2 garlic cloves minced

5 sage leaves

4 sprigs of thyme

2 celery sprig leaves

1 bay leaf

1 carrot chopped or 72g

1/2 onion chopped or 74g

4 cups or 1000ml turkey stock

Gravy

2 tbsp or 28g unsalted butter

2 tbsp or 16g all-purpose flour

1 cup or 250ml giblet stock reduction

Giblets chopped (liver, heart, and gizzard)

2 hard-boiled eggs diced

1 cup or 250ml turkey pan drippings (3/4 cup water added to the turkey roasting pan)

1/2 cup or 125ml heavy cream

Salt and pepper to taste

Giblet prep work:

Remove the neck, heart, liver and gizzard from the turkey. Check the gizzard to see if any hard parts need to be cut off. Put the liver in a container and place in the refrigerator. Then place the heart, gizzard and neck in a saucepot along with all the giblet stock ingredients. Bring to a simmer, then turn the heat to low and reduce uncovered for 1.5 to 2 hours. When there is 30 minutes of cooking time left, add the liver to the pot.

Fill a second saucepot with water. Bring to a boil and then add 2 eggs. Cook for 8 minutes. Place the eggs into an ice bath.

Remove the giblets from the pan and strain the stock into a fat separator or bowl. Dice the heart, gizzard, liver, eggs and pull the meat from the neck.

To make the roux for the gravy:

Add butter to a saucepan over medium heat and melt down. Then add flour. Stir and cook over low to medium heat for roughly 5 minutes until the roux (flour butter mixture) is a blonde color. Set to the side and let it cool in the pan.

To make the Gravy:

Take the turkey out of the oven. Remove the turkey from the baking pan – cover and let it rest in a warm place. Put the pan on a stove burner over low heat and deglaze it by adding water. Scrape the bottom of the baking pan to incorporate the pan drippings into the liquid. Once all the drippings are incorporated into the liquid, remove from heat and strain the liquid into a fat separator or bowl.

Put the saucepan with the cool roux (butter flour mixture) on a burner – don't turn on the heat yet.

Combine the dripping liquid and giblet poaching liquid together in a fat separator or bowl. Check to see how much liquid you have. You will need at least 2 cups or 500ml of warm cooking liquid to make this gravy.

Add the warm/hot cooking liquid to the saucepan on the burner with the cool roux, mix, turn on the heat to medium, and bring to a simmer. Then reduce the heat to low. Skim the top to remove any impurities/foam. Cook for roughly 8-10 minutes, then add heavy cream and the giblets. Mix, bring to a simmer. Reduce over low heat until it is as thick as you would like.

Taste and adjust the seasoning – add salt and pepper as needed.

Recipe video tutorial

https://youtu.be/_V7TJpHOojE

GREEN BEAN CASSEROLE

Makes 6 to 8 servings

Ingredients:

1 lb. green beans

4 tbsp or 56g unsalted butter (1 tbsp or 14g to cook the onions and 3 tbsp or 42g to make the roux)

2 to 3 tbsp 15 to 30ml neutral oil

1 onion diced

12 button mushrooms

2 cloves of garlic

3 tbsp or 24g all-purpose flour

2.5 cups or 625ml heavy cream

1 tsp black pepper

1 tsp chicken bouillon

1/2 tbsp or 7ml Worcestershire sauce

Salt to taste

Handful of fried onions (optional)

Cook the green beans, strain them, and put them to the side.

Add 1 tbsp butter and 1 tbsp neutral oil to a large saucepan over medium to high heat. Once hot, add the onion and sauté until lightly browned around the edges.

Add mushrooms and cook until they are tender (add more oil if needed).

Once the mushrooms and onions are cooked, add the garlic and cook for 30 seconds.

Make a well in the center of the pan and add 3 tbsp or 42g butter, melt it, then add flour, mix, and cook for 2 to 3 minutes.

Pour in heavy cream, mix, scrape the bottom and sides of the pan to release any bits and pieces. Add black pepper, chicken bouillon, and Worcestershire sauce. Bring to a simmer over medium heat and cook for 5 minutes or until thick. Taste the sauce and add salt and pepper if needed.

To make the casserole:

Butter a baking dish (for this recipe, use an 8x8" or size 12 au gratin dish), add the green beans, pour the sauce on top and spread it evenly over the beans.

Bake in a pre-heated oven at 350° F or 176° C uncovered for 40 minutes.

(Optional) Take the casserole out of the oven and add fried onions on top and bake for 2-10 minutes more or until the onions are golden brown.

Recipe video tutorial

https://youtu.be/5IildZu9D9s

HASHBROWN CASEROLE

Makes 6 to 8 servings

Ingredients:

5 tbsp or 75g bacon grease or unsalted butter

1.5 cups or 185g chopped sweet onion

1/4 tsp garlic powder

1/4 tsp ground mustard

Dash of black pepper

1/4 cup or 32g all-purpose flour

3/4 cup or 187ml chicken broth

3/4 cup or 187ml heavy cream

Dash of Worcestershire sauce

1/2 cup or 135g sour cream

2 cups or 226g shredded cheddar cheese (1 cup for the sauce and 1 cup for topping the casserole)

30z or 850g pack of frozen shredded hashbrowns – thawed

Green onion or chives to garnish (optional)

To make the sauce:

To a Dutch oven over medium to high heat, add the bacon grease. Once melted, add the chopped onions, cook until tender.

Add a dash of garlic powder, ground mustard, and black pepper, stir, cook for 30 seconds.

Whisk in the flour and cook over medium heat for 2 to 3 minutes.

Pour in chicken stock, mix and then add the heavy cream and Worcestershire sauce. Cook over medium heat until thick, stirring frequently.

Take the sauce off heat and add 1 cup or 113g of shredded cheddar cheese. Stir it well into the sauce. Then mix in the sour cream.

Taste the sauce and add salt or pepper if needed.

To make the casserole:

Add one 30z bag of frozen shredded hashbrowns that has been thawed to the sauce, mix well then top with 1 cup of cheddar cheese.

Bake in a pre-heated over at 350°F or 176°C uncovered for 45 minutes to 50 minutes. Then turn the heat up to 450°F or 230°C. Cook for 5 minutes or until the top of the casserole is lightly golden brown.

Recipe video tutorial

https://youtu.be/zCg21vXX_Pl

TURKEY DRIPPINGS GRAVY

Makes 4 to 6 servings

Ingredients:

2 cups or 500ml of turkey stock (you can also use chicken stock or even water)

3 tbsp or 42g unsalted butter

3 tbsp or 24g all-purpose flour

Dash of salt and pepper

To harvest the turkey drippings:

Cook the turkey on a baking pan (preferably with a rack). Remove the turkey and place the baking pan on a burner (or two) over low to medium heat.

Add the turkey stock to the pan. Use a flat bottom spatula to scrape the bottom and sides of the pan to release the turkey drippings into the cooking liquid.

Once the drippings are incorporated into the liquid, remove the pan from heat and strain the cooking liquid into a glass bowl or fat separator.

To make the gravy:

Add butter (or use the fat separated from the drippings if you're using a fat separator) to a saucepan over medium heat. When the butter is melted, whisk in the flour, cook for roughly 10 minutes over medium heat until the roux (butter and flour mixture) is blonde in color.

While whisking, pour the turkey dripping liquid into the pan, cook for 5 to 10 minutes or until the gravy is as thick as you would like. Occasionally skim the top of the gravy to remove any foam/impurities.

Taste the gravy to see if you need to adjust the seasoning – add salt or pepper as needed.

Recipe video tutorial

https://youtu.be/z66z_nXmyks

LOADED CRANBERRY SAUCE

Makes 2 cups or 500ml

Ingredients:

1/2 cup or 125ml orange juice

3/4 cup or 175g light brown sugar

1 lb. or 16oz cranberries

1/2 cup or 125ml Tawny Port

1/2 tsp allspice

1/2 cup dehydrated blueberries

Zest of half an orange

Half an apple peeled and diced

Salt and pepper

Pour orange juice and brown sugar into a saucepan, mix and then turn the heat to medium. Dissolve the brown sugar.

Add the cranberries and bring the sauce to a simmer. Cover it with a lid and cook for 10 minutes.

Occasionally, use a spoon or spatula to smash a few of the cranberries.

Add the Tawny Port, allspice, blueberries, orange zest, and diced apples. Mix and simmer for 5 minutes more or until the sauce is as thick as you would like – note that the sauce will look thin while hot, but it will thicken up when it cools.

Add a dash of salt and pepper, stir.

Pour into a serving bowl and let the sauce cool. Cover with plastic wrap and place into the refrigerator until ready to serve.

Recipe video tutorial

https://youtu.be/LWjRvrSstEs

DESSERT SAUCES

Indulge in the sweet symphony of flavors as you explore the delectable world of Dessert Sauces. This chapter is a journey into the enticing universe of sauces meticulously crafted to transform ordinary desserts into extraordinary culinary delights. From a mouthwatering Guinness chocolate topping sauce that cascades over a decadent brownie to the fruity allure of a vibrant blueberry sauce drizzled atop creamy ice cream, these sauces are the finishing touch that elevates the dessert experience. Whether you crave the classic elegance of caramel sauce, the zesty kick of a citrus glaze, or the decadent richness of butterscotch sauce, this curated collection caters to every sweet tooth. Delve into the art of saucing desserts, where each recipe adds a burst of flavor, texture, and visual appeal. Get ready to embark on a journey that celebrates the transformative power of dessert sauces, turning the ordinary into the extraordinary, one luscious drizzle at a time.

ORANGE DESSERT SAUCE

Makes 1/2 cup or 125ml

Ingredients:

4 oranges (3 for juicing – 1 cup or 250ml and 1 for the zest and orange segments)

1/4 cup or 55g granulated white sugar

1/2 tsp cornstarch

1 tbsp or 15ml Brandy

1 tbsp or 15ml Grenadine

1 tbsp or 14g cold unsalted butter

Zest half an orange- try not to get any of the white pith.

Segment the zested orange by removing the peel, white pith and orange membrane. Place the segmented orange into a bowl. Squeeze the remaining orange membrane over the bowl to retain any residual juice.

Juice 3 oranges – for roughly 1 cup or 250 ml.

Make a cornstarch slurry by mixing the cornstarch with 1 tbsp or 15 ml of the orange juice. Set to the side.

To make the sauce:

Pour the orange juice and granulated sugar into a saucepan. Turn the heat to medium, stir and dissolve the sugar.

Add the orange segments, orange zest, and stir in the cornstarch slurry. Bring to a simmer and turn the heat to low. Reduce for 20 minutes or roughly by half.

Stir in the Brandy and Grenadine, cook for 1 to 2 minutes.

Turn off the heat and add the cold butter, stirring with a spoon. Once melted, you are ready to serve!

Recipe video tutorial

https://youtu.be/OKKDVG-Drlg

BLUEBERRY
TOPPING SAUCE

Makes 2 cups or 500ml

Ingredients:

1 cup or 250ml of water

2 cups or 285g fresh blueberries

1 cup or 220g granulated white sugar

1/2 tsp ground ginger

1/2 tsp vanilla extract

1/2 tsp lemon juice

Cornstarch slurry

1 tbsp or 8g cornstarch

1 tbsp or 15ml of water

Add 1 cup water and the blueberries to a saucepot Turn the heat to medium, and mix in the sugar and ground ginger. Bring to a simmer, then turn the heat to low and cook for 5 to 8 minutes uncovered.

Make a cornstarch slurry- in a small bowl, mix together the cornstarch and water. Set to the side.

Pour the vanilla and lemon juice into the pot. Mix and then stir in the cornstarch slurry (make sure to give the slurry a quick stir before mixing it into the sauce). Turn the heat to medium-high, bring it to a simmer and cook for 30 seconds or until thick.

Recipe video tutorial

https://youtu.be/wLz2J1JXJeo

BUTTERSCOTCH TOPPING SAUCE

Makes 3/4 cup or 187ml

Ingredients:

1/4 cup or 60g unsalted butter

3/4 cup or 150g dark brown sugar

1/2 tsp lemon juice

1/2 cup or 125ml heavy cream

1/2 tsp vanilla extract

1/2 tsp salt

Melt the butter in a saucepan over medium heat. Add the dark brown sugar, mix, and add the lemon juice. Stir frequently over medium heat. At first, the sauce will be liquid, but the sugar will not dissolve. Then, the sauce will become clumpy and lumpy, keep stirring. After 5 to 10 minutes, the sauce will return to a liquid consistency again and the sugar will be fully dissolved.

Once the sugar has dissolved, whisk in the heavy cream. The sauce will spit and sputter, but keep stirring until it stops. Be careful not to burn yourself.

Take the sauce off heat, add the vanilla and salt, and stir.

Let the sauce cool a bit and you're ready to dive in!

Recipe video tutorial

https://youtu.be/1tYxZMDQGms

CARAMEL COFFEE SAUCE

Makes 2 cups or 500ml

Ingredients:

1.5 cups or 330g granulated white sugar

1/4 cup or 63ml water

1 cup or 250ml heavy cream

1 tsp instant coffee

5 tbsp or 70g unsalted butter

1/2 tsp salt

Warm the heavy cream and add the instant coffee (1 tsp or more if you like a stronger coffee taste) in a small saucepot. Dissolve the coffee and put the pot to the side.

To another high-sided saucepot, add the sugar and water, and turn the heat up to medium-high. Use a basting brush and some water to remove any dry sugar from touching the side of the pot. Cook for roughly 10 minutes or until the sugar is melted and turns an amber color.

Take the saucepot with the sugar off the burner and whisk in the warm cream/coffee mixture. The sauce will spit and sputter, so be careful not to burn yourself while whisking. Once the cream is well combined and the sauce has stopped bubbling, add the cold butter off heat, stir and dissolve it into the sauce.

Put the sauce back on the burner, turn the heat to low, bring to a simmer and cook for 30 seconds to 1 minute. Turn off the heat and mix in the salt.

Let the sauce slightly cool before serving.

Recipe video tutorial

https://youtu.be/COYmZFJp8As

CHERRY AND PORT DESSERT SAUCE

Makes 1 ½ cups or 375ml

Ingredients:

2 cups or 327g frozen cherries

1 tbsp or 15ml lemon juice

1 tbsp or 14g unsalted butter

1 tsp vanilla extract

1/4 cup or 63ml water

1/4 cup or 63ml Tawny Port

1/2 cup or 110g granulated white sugar

1 cinnamon stick

1 star anise

Cornstarch Slurry

1 tbsp or 8g cornstarch

1/4 cup or 63ml water

To a saucepan, add the cherries, water, Tawny Port, and sugar, and stir. Then turn heat on to medium. Drop in the star anise, cinnamon, lemon juice, butter, and vanilla extract. Bring to a boil, turn the heat down and simmer the sauce for 5 to 8 minutes.

Make the cornstarch slurry: mix 1/4 cup or 63ml water and 1 tbsp cornstarch. Set it aside for later.

Take the cinnamon stick and star anise out of the saucepan. Give the cornstarch slurry a quick mix and stir it into the sauce. Bring the sauce back to a simmer and take it off heat when the sauce thickens up.

Recipe video tutorial

https://youtu.be/d4Nha2KuxH0

CHOCOLATE BRANDY SAUCE

Makes 1 cup or 250ml

Ingredients:

3/4 cup or 187ml heavy cream

3 tbsp or 45g light brown sugar

2 tbsp or 30ml Brandy

Pinch of salt

4 oz or 114g bittersweet chocolate

Chop the chocolate into small chunks and place into a mixing bowl.

To a saucepan, add the heavy cream, brown sugar, salt, and Brandy. Mix over medium heat until the ingredients have dissolved and the cream is just starting to bubble and steam.

Pour the warm cream mixture into the bowl with the chocolate. Make sure to submerge all the chocolate in the creamy liquid. Let it sit for 2 to 5 minutes until the chocolate has melted.

Whisk until smooth and you're ready to enjoy!

Recipe video tutorial

https://youtu.be/HCCV9Js0кс0

HOT FUDGE TOPPING SAUCE

Makes 3/4 cup or 187ml

Ingredients:

5oz or 141g bittersweet chocolate 60% cacao

1/2 cup or 125ml heavy cream

1 tbsp or 8g powdered sugar

1/4 tsp cayenne pepper

1 tsp vanilla extract

Chop the chocolate into small pieces and place them into a mixing bowl.

To a saucepan, add the heavy cream and warm over medium heat until the cream just starts to steam.

Pour the warm cream into the mixing bowl with the chocolate. Use a spoon or spatula to make sure the chocolate is fully covered and let it sit for 2 to 5 minutes.

Mix with a spatula or whisk. Once smooth, add the powdered sugar, cayenne pepper, and vanilla extract. Give it a stir, and you're ready to serve!

Recipe video tutorial

https://youtu.be/SsuikNBdxgY

GUINNESS CHOCOLATE SAUCE

Makes 2 cups 500ml

Ingredients:

1.5 cups or 270g semi-sweet chocolate – 56% cacao

1 cup or 250ml Guinness extra stout beer

3/4 cup or 165g granulated white sugar

1/2 cup or 35g unsweetened cocoa powder

1/4 tsp salt

Dash of cayenne pepper

2 tsp vanilla extract

Chop the chocolate into small pieces and put it to the side.

Pour the Guinness into a saucepan, add the sugar and cocoa powder. Stir, turn the heat to medium and bring to a simmer. Cook for 5 minutes.

Turn off the heat, add the chopped chocolate to the saucepan. Make sure the chocolate is submerged in the warm liquid. Let it sit for 2 to 5 minutes, then pour in the vanilla extract and (optional) a dash of cayenne pepper.

Stir and you're ready to dive in!

Recipe video tutorial

https://youtu.be/5BJFKDHZOIE

KAHLUA CARAMEL SAUCE

Makes 1 cup or 250ml

Ingredients:

3/4 cup or 165g granulated white sugar

1/8 cup or 32ml water

1 tsp lemon juice

1/2 cup or 125ml heavy cream

2 tbsp or 28g unsalted butter

Pinch of salt

1 tbsp or 15ml Kahlua

1 tbsp or 15ml orange liqueur

Add sugar, water, and lemon juice to a saucepot. Shimmy and shake the pot to mix the water/lemon juice into the sugar. Bring to a simmer over medium to high heat. Once the liquid starts to simmer, turn the heat to low and cook for 10 minutes or until the liquid turns an amber color – don't stir.

Take the pan off heat and whisk in the heavy cream. The sauce will spit and sputter, so be careful not to burn yourself – keep whisking. Once it stops bubbling, put the pot back on the burner and heat on medium-low, stir, and bring back to a light simmer.

Take the pot off heat once it starts to simmer, add the butter, stir it into the caramel.

Add the salt, Kahlua, and orange liqueur, and mix. Let it slightly cool and you're ready to serve!

Recipe video tutorial

https://youtu.be/SavrvsDB-t0

Printed in Great Britain
by Amazon

47987491R10080